Feb 2019

CALIFORNIA

The Golden State

Anna Maria Johnson, Michael Burgan,
and William McGeveran

Cavendish

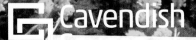

Published in 2019 by Cavendish Square Publishing, LLC
243 5th Avenue, Suite 136, New York, NY 10016

Fourth Edition

Website: cavendishsq.com

This publication represents the opinions and views of the author based on his or her personal experience, knowledge, and research. The information in this book serves as a general guide only. The author and publisher have used their best efforts in preparing this book and disclaim liability rising directly or indirectly from the use and application of this book.

All websites were available and accurate when this book was sent to press.

Library of Congress Cataloging-in-Publication Data

Names: Johnson, Anna Maria, author. | Burgan, Michael, author. | McGeveran, William, author.
Title: California : the Golden State / Anna Maria Johnson, Michael Burgan, and William McGeveran.
Description: Fourth edition. | New York : Cavendish Square, [2019] | Series:
It's my state! | Includes bibliographical references and index. | Audience: Grades 3-5.
Identifiers: LCCN 2017048030 (print) | LCCN 2018000859 (ebook) | ISBN 9781502626219 (ebook) |
ISBN 9781502626257 (library bound) | ISBN 9781502644381 (pbk.)
Subjects: LCSH: California--Juvenile literature. | California--Civilization--Juvenile literature.
Classification: LCC F861.3 (ebook) | LCC F861.3 .B87 2019 (print) | DDC 979.4--dc23
LC record available at https://lccn.loc.gov/2017048030

Editorial Director: David McNamara
Editor: Caitlyn Miller
Copy Editor: Nathan Heidelberger
Associate Art Director: Alan Sliwinski
Designer: Jessica Nevins
Production Coordinator: Karol Szymczuk
Photo Research: J8 Media

Printed in the United States of America

It's My STATE!

Table of Contents

SNAPSHOT
CALIFORNIA

The Golden State

State Flag

California's flag is based on an older flag design called the Bear Flag. That flag was used for the Bear Flag Revolt in 1846. California's settlers at that time decided they did not want to be controlled by Mexico anymore. They raised this flag over a fort in Sonoma. After California became part of the United States, the bear flag was adopted as its state flag in 1911 to help remember its past. The grizzly bear represents strength. The red star refers to Texas, the Lone Star State. Texas and California, along with some other states in the southwest, were once part of Mexico before they joined the United States.

Statehood

September 9, 1850

Population

39,536,653
(2017 census estimate)

Capital

Sacramento

State Song

California's state song is called "I Love You, California" by F. B. Silverwood. It was the official song of California's world's fair in 1915. The song was also played on the first ship that passed through the Panama Canal. (The Panama Canal was completed in 1914.)

HISTORICAL EVENTS TIMELINE

1542
European explorer Juan Rodríguez Cabrillo reaches California.

1826
Jedediah Smith brings the first United States citizens to California by land.

1846
The Mexican-American War begins over territory disputes. By the war's end in 1848, California becomes a US territory.

State Seal

California's state seal includes the state motto, Eureka! It means, "I found it!" in Greek. The phrase calls to mind one of California's most exciting moments in history, when gold was found in 1848. The seal also shows thirty-one stars. They represent that California became the thirty-first state in the United States.

State Tree

The state tree is the California redwood. Redwoods grow along the state's north and central coasts. People can see many of these huge trees in California's Redwood National and State Parks. One redwood deep in the forest there is said to be the tallest known tree in the world. It is over 379 feet (115.5 meters) tall. Its location is kept secret so people will not disturb it.

California redwoods grow to an astonishing height.

State Flower

The California poppy (*Eschscholzia californica*) grows wild in many parts of the state. The blossoms can be yellow or orange, almost like the color of gold. The golden poppy became the official state flower in 1903.

1849

The gold rush attracts settlers from the East Coast and from as far away as China.

1850

California becomes the thirty-first state in the Union.

1937

The Golden Gate Bridge opens to the public.

State
Animal
Grizzly Bear

State
Insect

**Dogface
Butterfly**

2000
An electricity crisis
causes blackouts
in California.

2003
Arnold Schwarzenegger
takes office as governor
after Californians
vote to remove Gray
Davis from office.

2011
A new law allows
undocumented
immigrants to receive
state aid for college.

State Marine Mammal
Gray Whale

State Reptile
Desert Tortoise

CURRENT EVENTS TIMELINE

2015

Wildfires burn 880,899 acres (356,487 hectares) of California land and destroy over 1,400 homes.

2017

California **invests** in new programs to save energy and reduce waste after the federal government cuts the Environmental Protection Agency's funding.

2018

In the aftermath of serious wildfires and heavy rains, deadly mudslides strike Southern California.

Big Sur is a region that stretches along 100 miles (160 kilometers) of California's coast.

1 Geography

California could be described as the richest state in the nation. Not only does it have the largest economy in the country, it also produces one-fourth of the food that Americans eat every day. The state is rich in natural features such as majestic mountains, giant forests, coastal plains, and great deserts. Modern riches include new technology such as electric cars, aeronautics, and power plants powered by the sun. And we can't forget the movies and celebrities!

California is also very big. It is the third-largest state, after Alaska and Texas. The state stretches along most of the continental United States' western coast. California is almost 800 miles (1,300 kilometers) long and about 250 miles (400 km) wide. It has a land area of almost 156,000 square miles (400,000 square kilometers). It is about 150 times bigger than the smallest state, Rhode Island.

The state is divided into fifty-eight counties. The biggest in population is Los Angeles County, which has more than ten million people. This is more people than any other county in the United States has. Sacramento is the state capital. It is in Sacramento County in the central part of the state. Within its borders, California holds a

California borders the US states of Oregon, Nevada, and Arizona. California also borders Mexico.

Sacramento has been the capital of California since 1854.

number of major geographic regions with many kinds of land, climate, plants, and animals.

The Mighty Mountains

Six different mountain regions cover just over half of California's land. The highest and largest range is the Sierra Nevada. The name is Spanish for "snowy range." Located in the eastern part of the state, the Sierra Nevada includes Mount Whitney. At 14,505 feet (4,421 meters), it is the tallest peak in the United States outside Alaska. High in the Sierras is Lake Tahoe, which also extends into Nevada. It is the second-deepest freshwater lake in the United States. (Crater Lake

The mountains of the Sierra Nevada are famous for their beauty.

in Oregon is the deepest.) In the winter, people come to Lake Tahoe and its shores to ski, snowboard, and ride toboggans. In the summer, tourists fish, hike, swim, water-ski, and sail.

Lake Tahoe boasts fun seasonal attractions.

In 1868, naturalist John Muir settled in California and closely studied the state's land. He called the Sierra Nevada "the most divinely beautiful of all the mountain chains I have ever seen." He also called it the "Range of Light." John Muir would later start one of the biggest environmental organizations in the world, the Sierra Club. His efforts helped preserve the Yosemite Valley, Sequoia National Park, and other areas. Many places in California are named after him. Natural attractions named in his honor include Muir Woods and Muir Beach.

John Muir lived from 1838 to 1914.

The Klamath Mountains rise in the northwest corner of California. These jagged peaks reach about 9,000 feet (2,740 m), and the slopes are covered with forests. Just east of the Klamath Mountains is the Cascade Range, which includes volcanoes. Mount Shasta is the largest of the volcanoes. The fifth-highest peak in California, Mount Shasta last erupted in 1786. Lassen Peak had a series of eruptions in more recent times, during 1914 through 1917. It is one of only two volcanoes in the continental United States that erupted during the twentieth century. The other is Mount Saint Helens in Washington State, which erupted on May 18, 1980.

Muir Woods National Monument

The Coast Ranges start just south of the Klamath Mountains. They stretch for about 400 miles (645 km) along the Pacific Ocean. The largest freshwater lake completely within the state, Clear Lake, is located within the Coast

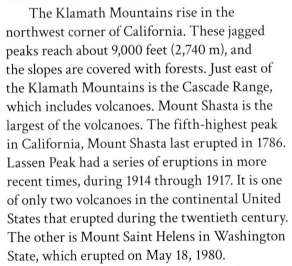

Mount Shasta became a National Landmark in 1976.

Ranges. Southern California has two smaller ranges, the Transverse and the Peninsular. The Peninsular Range includes smaller ranges, such as the Santa Ana Mountains, San Jacinto Mountains, and Santa Rosa Mountains. The Transverse is the only mountain chain in the state that runs from east to west.

FAST FACT

California's tallest point is Mount Whitney. At 14,505 feet (4,421 m), it's the tallest peak in the lower forty-eight states (the tallest peaks are in Alaska). Just 60 miles (96.5 km) away is Death Valley, the continent's lowest point at 282 feet (86 m) below sea level.

Moving Waters

The Central Valley sits between the Sierra Nevada and the Coast Ranges. According to the California Water Science Center, it covers an area of around 20,000 square miles (51,800 sq km). Millions of years ago, the Pacific Ocean covered that part of California. Mountains rose around the water. The water trapped between the mountains later broke through the Coast Ranges and emptied into what is now known as the San Francisco Bay. Later, huge sheets of ice covered parts of California. The last ice age in the region ended more than ten thousand years ago. Lakes formed by melting ice flooded the area once again. Today, however, the center of California is a huge valley.

In the nineteenth century, the remaining lakes and swamps in the region were drained so the land could be used for farming. Water control is used to prevent rivers, such as the Sacramento and San Joaquin, from overflowing during the spring snowmelt. Dams, such as the Shasta Dam, Don Pedro Dam, and Isabella Dam, were built to do this.

The Golden Gate Bridge straddles the San Francisco Bay.

The Central Valley is one of the best places on Earth for growing cereal grains, cotton, citrus, nuts, lettuce, tomatoes, grapes, and more than 250 other crops. The Central Valley produces crops worth about $17 billion per year. Almonds, in particular, are an important crop. There are around 6,500 almond farms in the state. In 2017, these farms were predicted to produce more than 2.2 billion pounds (997.9 million kg) of almonds.

Farmers rely on **irrigation** to water their crops. Canals and large waterways called aqueducts bring water from lakes and reservoirs to the fields. Many of them were part of the Central Valley Project. This was a project that began in the 1930s to provide and control water in the region.

There are around 6.5 million people living in the Central Valley, and it is one of the fastest-growing regions in the state. Many of California's major cities are located in the Central Valley,

The Shasta Dam

Explorers in California's Early History

When European explorers first arrived in California, they thought it might be the mythical island called "California" described in a Spanish book that was popular in the sixteenth century. At that time, truth and myth were hard to separate because of a lack of information. According to Garci Rodríguez de Montalvo's story, California was "an island on the right hand of the Indies … very close to the side of the Terrestrial Paradise." Their Queen Calafia was strong, courageous, and beautiful. The country was rich in gold and jewels.

By 1535, Hernán Cortés and his crew had arrived in what is now called Baja California (part of Mexico). They named the real place after the one in the story because they seemed to resemble one another. Later, explorers learned that California was not an island but a peninsula attached to the continent of North America. More than three hundred years later, people would discover that at least one part of the old myth of California—being rich in gold—was true!

California is a very large state that includes many kinds of geography: coastal plains, mountain ranges, deserts, and valleys. Early explorers and settlers set up homes and **missions** along the coast after arriving by boat. Because of the mountain ranges along the eastern edge, people had trouble reaching California by land. This is why it would take about three hundred more years before people would travel to California over land from the eastern United States. Deserts like the Great Basin and the Mojave Desert also kept early settlers from making a home in parts of the state.

Jessie Benton Frémont wrote a book about traveling to California with her famous politician husband, John, near the time when gold was first discovered. In it, she says:

When it was first planned that I should go to California, in the spring of 1848, the gold discoveries had not been made. In August of that year was the first finding, and with the uncertain, slow communications then had with that coast, it was nearly winter before the news reached us in Washington. It seems odd to recall now the little vial of gold-dust so carefully brought as voucher for the startling story. A long sail down the coast to Mazatlan, then the crossing through Mexico, then another sailing vessel to New Orleans, made the chance mail-route: only a strong party could risk itself overland, and few ventured into the winter.

including Sacramento, Fresno, Bakersfield, and Stockton.

This population growth has led to a large traffic problem between the valley, where many people live, and major cities where many people work. San Francisco and Los Angeles, in particular, face this problem. Some residents choose to take turns carpooling in order to reduce the number of cars on the road and relieve some of the stress of driving through the valley every day.

Traffic is a source of frustration for Los Angeles commuters.

Desert Regions

Hot, dry desert regions cover much of the southern part of the state. The Great Basin is a vast dry area that extends east of the Sierra Nevada and across the border into Nevada. It contains Death Valley. One spot in Death Valley National Park is 282 feet (86 m) below sea level— the lowest point in the United States. The valley's fascinating sand dunes and rock formations attract many visitors. The Mojave Desert is just south of Death Valley. South of the Mojave is the Colorado Desert, which extends into Mexico.

Within the Colorado Desert is the Imperial Valley. Although the valley receives little rainfall, it is a major center of agriculture. The All-American Canal carries water to the valley from the Colorado River, which flows along California's southeast border with Arizona.

Also in this region is the Salton Sea, which is saltier than the Pacific Ocean. The salt comes from the soil in nearby valleys. The Salton Sea formed by accident. In 1905, heavy floods caused irrigation canals from the Colorado River to burst, and a valley filled with water.

A Two-Season Climate

California has two seasons: dry and rainy. But temperatures and rainfall in California vary greatly from region to region. Along the southern coast, people enjoy warm, sunny weather almost all year long. Temperatures are cooler on the northern coast, which gets more rainfall. The San Francisco area is famous for its fog, which rolls in from the ocean on summer mornings and evenings. The Central Valley is hot and dry in the summer. In the winter, the temperature drops and the air becomes humid. The mountains also have warm summers and rainy winters. Higher peaks, such as those in the Sierra Nevada, are covered with snow all winter long. The deserts are hot and dry, with little rainfall. At night, the temperature falls quickly.

Death Valley's unique features bring visitors to the desert.

Amazing Animals

The California Department of Fish and Wildlife lists more than 230 species of mammals and about 665 species of birds that find a home in California or in the Pacific Ocean just off the coast. There are at least forty-three species of salamanders, thirty-one kinds of frogs and toads, twelve types of turtles, and almost one hundred different species of lizards and snakes!

At times, San Francisco's fog can make it difficult to spot the Golden Gate Bridge.

Many animals live in the deserts. Most of them avoid the sun by staying in caves or under rocks during the day. Some, such as the kit fox, are nocturnal. This means they are awake at night and hunt for most of their food then. One animal that braves the day's powerful heat is the desert tortoise. These reptiles plod through the hills and sand looking for plants to eat. Then they return to their homes—snug holes called burrows that they have dug into the sand.

Hollywood and Other Top Attractions

In 1918, businessman Sid Grauman's first theater opened in Los Angeles. Grauman already owned theaters elsewhere in California, but the unique vision he brought to LA changed the face of Hollywood. Grauman's Chinese Theatre opened in 1927, and quickly became the site of major movie premieres. Then Grauman had the idea to honor movie stars by preserving their handprints and footprints in cement outside the theater. The Forecourt of the Stars had arrived. Today, the theater is known as the TCL Chinese Theatre. It remains a wildly popular place for premieres, and the Forecourt of the Stars is always expanding.

A similar attraction is just down the street from TCL. The Hollywood Walk of Fame opened in 1960. More than 2,500 stars line the Walk of Fame. Anyone can submit a nomination for their favorite star to be recognized, but very few nominations are selected. The Walk of Fame sees more than ten million visitors each year.

Outside of Hollywood, California boasts tourist hot spots of all kinds. Many of these sites center around the state's natural beauty. Its parks and beaches bring visitors from all over. In fact, California is one of the most popular surfing destinations in the world!

TCL Chinese Theatre

A surfer catches a wave at Huntington Beach.

California's Biggest Cities

(Population numbers are from the US Census Bureau's 2017 projections for incorporated cities.)

Los Angeles

1. Los Angeles: population 3,999,759

LA is best known for Hollywood, a district within the city. Many TV shows and movies are made there. Famous LA landmarks include the Hollywood Walk of Fame, the Griffith Observatory, and nearby Venice Beach.

2. San Diego: population 1,419,516

Beautiful weather, gorgeous beaches, and outdoor activities are just some of the reasons more than a million people call San Diego home. Located just north of the Mexico border, San Diego boasts opportunities for biking, hiking, surfing, and more.

3. San Jose: population 1,035,317

San Jose sits in an area nicknamed "Silicon Valley." This term refers to the large number of **silicon** chip manufacturers that were once located there. Now, many of the world's biggest technology companies are headquartered in or near San Jose.

4. San Francisco: population 884,363

Known as "The City by the Bay," San Francisco is a city full of sights to see and things to do. Some of the most famous landmarks in California are right there. You can ride a cable car, explore Golden Gate Park, or watch the sea lions at Pier 39!

5. Fresno: population 527,438

Fresno County, in central California, is the number-one agricultural producer in the United States. The area is known for its abundant produce. Fresno is also close to three major national parks: Yosemite, Sequoia, and Kings Canyon National Parks.

Fresno

6. Sacramento: population 501,901

Sacramento is the capital of California. Gold was discovered around 50 miles (80 km) northeast of the city, which led to the California gold rush. Sacramento quickly grew in size and population. Today, visitors can enjoy the capital's parks, museums, and riverfront.

7. Long Beach: population 469,450

Long Beach is a community located between Los Angeles and Orange County. The Port of Long Beach is one of the largest shipping ports in the world. The city is also home to the RMS *Queen Mary*, a retired ship that once transported troops during World War II. Today, you can tour the ship.

8. Oakland: population 425,195

Oakland sits across the bay from San Francisco. It is home to three professional sports teams: the Oakland Athletics (baseball), Oakland Raiders (football), and Golden State Warriors (basketball). There is also a large artist community there, along with parks and a lakefront (Lake Merritt).

9. Bakersfield: population 380,874

Bakersfield is the oil-producing capital of California. "The Bakersfield Sound," a twangy way of playing the steel guitar, was made famous by country singers Merle Haggard and Buck Owens during the 1950s.

Anaheim

10. Anaheim: population 352,497

Anaheim, located outside of Los Angeles, is best known for being the home of one of the most visited tourist attractions in the world: Disneyland.

A kit fox on the prowl

Bobcats, deer, beavers, foxes, skunks, and chipmunks are a few of the animals commonly found in California's forests. Bears, elk, and antelope live in northern and mountain areas. Sea lions and huge elephant seals live along the coast. A baby elephant seal gains about 10 pounds (4.5 kg) per day!

Many kinds of wildlife live on or near the Farallon Islands, off the coast of San Francisco. A big colony of elephant seals lives there. Whales pass by, and sharks live in the waters. Scientists are studying the sharks in the wild to learn more about these skilled sea hunters.

The eight Channel Islands, off the coast of Southern California, are home to an amazing assortment of plant and animal life, including playful sea otters. An underwater forest of kelp—giant seaweed—provides shelter for many kinds of fish. Porpoises often swim past the islands. In 1980, five of the Channel Islands became a US national park.

The Channel Islands

Our Responsibility to Wildlife

Humans can make life difficult for wildlife. Cars, power plants, and factories create air pollution. Chemicals sometimes run into rivers and streams. As cities and towns grow, people need more land for homes and businesses. All of these things can endanger, or threaten to wipe out, different kinds of plants and animals.

Several of the state's well-known birds are endangered. With a wingspan of more than 9 feet (3 m), the California condor is the largest land bird in North America. Condors live in cliffs, under big rocks, or inside holes in trees. The number of condors in the wild fell after the 1940s because of lead contamination. Scientists then began a program to increase their numbers. More than four hundred condors are alive today, compared with just twenty-three in 1982. In 2001, a California condor chick was born in the wild. It was the first wild condor birth in seventeen years.

Giving animals **legal** protection is one way to help save them. But some people argue against such laws. The effort to protect the spotted owl in Washington, Oregon, and California during the 1990s is one example. These birds are considered endangered in the Pacific Northwest and threatened farther south. Some people want to reduce logging to protect the forests where they live. Others say this hurts lumber companies and takes away people's jobs. Laws to protect nature have created some new jobs, however, in fields like biology, conservation, and recreation.

About one out of eight Americans lives in California. Perhaps this is no surprise when we consider the richness, beauty, and challenges of this western coast of the United States. People have settled here to enjoy the natural beauty of mountains, deserts, forests, and the coast. Using creativity and problem-solving skills, people have made changes to the landscape to make it suit their needs and wishes. Over time, people are learning the importance of protecting the plants and animals that also make their home in California.

FAST FACT

News of the gold discovery in California took around seven months to reach the East Coast. At the time, traveling by land was nearly impossible. The news had to travel by boat around South America—a journey of 17,000 miles (27,350 km)!

What Lives in California?

Flora

California Poppy The California poppy grows wild throughout the state. It is also called the flame flower. The California poppy became the state flower in 1903.

California Sagebrush The California sagebrush thrives in drier regions and helps to control erosion on sloping land. Birds, amphibians, reptiles, and small mammals use sagebrush communities as their homes. The Luiseño Native Americans used it in ceremonies. Miners used it in their beds to control fleas.

Joshua Tree Some people think that the unusual Joshua tree looks like something from a Dr. Seuss book. A good place to visit them is Joshua Tree National Park, located where two deserts (the Mojave and the Colorado) meet.

Joshua tree

Lace Lichen Lace lichen (*Ramalina menziesii*) is not technically a plant, but it does grow on trees. Lichens are made of a fungus and an alga. Lace lichen looks like lace or hair draped over branches. It became California's official state lichen on January 1, 2016.

Redwoods California is well known for its redwood forests. One is the Jedediah Smith Redwood State Park, named for the first white explorer to reach California by land. The coast redwood and the giant sequoia need high rainfall to reach their lofty heights. The tallest reaches over 379 feet (115.5 m)!

Fauna

California Condor The California condor represents one of the best successes of conservation efforts. After their population dropped to just 22 in the world, people worked to save them from extinction. As of 2016, there were 446 in the world, including 276 living in the wild.

California condor

California Tiger Salamander The California tiger salamander is a special kind of amphibian that lives in the Central Valley and other areas. Their tails appear tiger-striped, while their bodies are black with yellow or white polka dots. They need wetlands to survive.

Gila monster

Gila Monster The Gila monster (pronounced "HEE-la" monster) is the only venomous lizard native to the United States. It was also the first venomous creature to be protected. Some people might wonder why we should protect a venomous animal, but without them, the ecosystem would change.

Island Foxes Island foxes are smaller than other foxes because they adapted to life in small habitats on the Channel Islands. Once nearly extinct, today they are no longer endangered. According to National Public Radio, "Officials say the Island foxes' recovery is the fastest of any mammal ever listed under the Endangered Species Act."

Walking Stick A very interesting California invertebrate is the walking stick. These insects look like a twig! California has twenty-one different species of the genus *Timema* living in the state, each adapted to blend in with a different and particular kind of plant.

Experts believe that the Chumash cave paintings found in California were created more than four hundred years ago.

2 The History of California

C alifornia historian Kevin Starr writes in his book *California: A History* that "if there is such a thing as DNA codes for states ... then crucial to the [heritage] of California would be ethnic diversity." California's story can only be told by exploring the many different groups and cultures that have made the Golden State what it is today. The Native peoples, Russians, Spanish, Mexicans, Japanese, Chinese, and early Americans and African Americans all played vital roles in California's development. More recently, about one-fourth of Californians are immigrants.

The first humans arrived in California more than ten thousand years ago. They probably came from northern Asia to Alaska, in small boats or over a strip of land that used to connect the two continents in the north. Eventually, some of these people traveled down the Pacific coast and settled in present-day California.

Many different Native American tribes called California their home. They included the

FAST FACT
Women could vote in California before they could vote in most other states. California was among nine western states that passed women's suffrage legislation by 1912, allowing women the right to vote within their state. Not until 1920 did the federal government pass the Nineteenth Amendment, granting all women nationwide the right to vote.

Sir Francis Drake explored California in the 1500s.

Chumash, who paddled wooden canoes, and the Pomo, who made beautiful baskets. Most communities had only a few hundred people, but some were larger. These Native tribes usually hunted, fished, and gathered nuts and seeds for their food. There was usually enough food to go around, so most tribes were peaceful. Wars were rare.

The Spanish Arrive

Experts estimate that about three hundred thousand Native Americans were living in present-day California in the 1500s. Their lives began to change when Europeans came to California. The Spanish were the first to arrive. In 1542, Juan Rodríguez Cabrillo, a Portuguese sailor exploring on behalf of Spain, sailed northward from Mexico. He was the first European to explore California's coast. Explorers took the name for the area from Garci Rodríguez de Montalvo's Spanish **fable**, in which a land called California was said to have gold and magical beasts.

A statue honoring Father Serra stands in Santa Barbara.

Nearly forty years later, the English explorer and pirate Sir Francis Drake sailed along California's coast and landed for a time to have his ship repaired. He established friendly relations with the local Natives.

However, Europeans did not settle in California until almost two hundred years later. The first Europeans to live in the region were mostly Spanish missionaries who had come to the New World to convert Native Americans to the Roman Catholic religion. In 1769, Father Junípero Serra built a mission, a settlement for carrying on his work. Named San Diego de Alcalá, it was the first of twenty-one missions to be built by the

Spanish in California. The missions covered large areas of land and made many products.

Today, Fort Ross is designated as a Historic State Park.

Serra and other missionaries taught the Native Americans how to raise crops and cattle, ride horses, and practice trades such as carpentry and weaving. But they often treated the Native American people like children. Missionaries made Native Americans give up their own traditions and forced them to work at the missions.

Russian fur traders, who came down from Alaska, also lived in California for a time. In 1812, the Russians built a fort north of San Francisco. Called Fort Ross, the settlement lasted until 1841.

Mexican Independence

In 1821, Mexico won its independence from Spain. California became part of the new nation, but the people of California were used to living and working without much outside control. Mexico sent governors to rule California, but they often clashed with the Californians. The Mexican government began to close down the missions, giving the mission lands to ranchers and Spanish people who had power. Many Native Americans were forced to work for the new owners under cruel conditions.

FAST FACT

Today there are more Spanish speakers in California than in Uruguay. In fact, the United States is second only to Mexico in having the most Spanish speakers! Metropolitan Los Angeles alone has more than 4 million Spanish speakers, while the nation of Uruguay has a total population of just 3.5 million (as of 2017).

California's First Peoples

California was inhabited long before Europeans set foot on its soil. Many different Native American tribes lived throughout the region. There were a variety of cultures. Some of the tribes include the Chumash, the Hupa, the Mojave, the Pomo, and the Ohlone. Each tribe had its own unique way of life that is an important part of the culture of California.

Many of the tribes traveled from place to place. Most of their houses were not meant to be permanent. They lived off the land, fishing, hunting, and gathering. Often tribes would move in search of new food. One of the many foods that many different tribes ate was acorns. Coastal tribes would eat shellfish. Tribes farther inland would gather berries and nuts, and sometimes farm. Most tribes in California cared deeply for nature. Animals, rivers, mountains, and stars were often important parts of their religions.

When the first Europeans arrived in California, they did not spend much time there. However, the Spanish eventually started the mission system and set up monasteries to capture and convert any Native Americans. Those who ran the missions did not give the Native people a choice about joining them. Land was taken away from different tribes. Many Native Americans died of European diseases including smallpox and cholera. Between the deaths from disease and the changes caused by the Spanish mission system, many different tribes lost their ways of life.

Fortunately, today there are many tribes in California who are dedicated to learning and connecting to their original traditions. There are so many federally recognized tribes in California that if they were listed here they would take up the whole page! A few of them are the California Valley Miwok Tribe, the Hoopa Valley Tribe, La Jolla Band of Luiseño Indians, and the Death Valley Timbi-Sha Shoshone Tribe. According to 2016 US census estimates, 1.7 percent of Californians identify as Native American.

An elder of the Chumash tribe keeps his heritage alive by performing a ceremony.

A Closer Look at the Chumash

The Chumash people were a Native American tribe that lived, and continue to live, along the coast of southern California. Some believe the tribe may have lived there as long as thirteen thousand years ago.

There were once more than twenty thousand Chumash. However, when the Spanish colonized the state in the 1700s, the Chumash population declined due to the spread of diseases that the Spanish brought with them. Here is a look at the Chumash culture.

Art: The Chumash drew pictographs, or symbol drawings, in caves along the California coast. It is not known what they mean. However, visitors can still see some of them at the Chumash Painted Cave Historic Park in Santa Barbara.

Currency: The name Chumash is thought to mean "ones who make shell bead money." This is because the Chumash used beads made from snail shells as currency. The value of a bead depended on the rarity of the shell and how much time was spent making it.

Music: Music was an important part of the Chumash culture. They sang songs of joy, songs that taught children lessons about right and wrong, and songs to help cure the sick.

Games: One game that the Chumash played was very similar to modern-day field hockey. Each team had a goal on one end of a rectangular playing field. The purpose of the game was for players to hit a small wooden ball into the other team's goal. This game was called shinny.

American Pioneers Arrive

In 1826, an American fur trapper named Jedediah Smith led a group of traders that reached California by crossing the Mojave Desert. They were the first settlers to arrive by land from the east. Over time, more Americans came on wagon trains. These pioneers had heard that the area had plenty of excellent land. In 1848, they learned that it also had plenty of gold.

A Swiss pioneer named John Sutter owned land near Sacramento. A carpenter named James Marshall was hired to build a mill for Sutter. In January 1848, Marshall found gold on the property. Soon people were rushing to Sutter's land in a "gold rush" that would change California forever.

Meanwhile, the United States had defeated Mexico in a war that began in 1846. On February 2, 1848, the two countries signed a treaty. California and other Mexican territory (including present-day Nevada, Utah, and parts of four other states) became part of the United States.

This painting shows Jedediah Smith and his band of settlers crossing the Mojave Desert.

Becoming a State

The California gold rush ended in 1855.

California's gold attracted people from all over the world. Almost ninety thousand people arrived in 1849. In the years that followed, hundreds of thousands more came to California. The newcomers, often called forty-niners, hoped to get rich. A few did make a fortune. However, most found nothing. Still, many thousands of them stayed in California and helped it grow.

In September 1850, California officially became a US state. It was admitted as a Free State, where people could not own or trade slaves. At that time, San Francisco was becoming California's most important city. It had a good harbor and was near the hills where gold had been found. Prior to the gold rush, the city had a tiny population. By 1852, more than thirty-five thousand people lived in San Francisco. The forty-niners needed food, clothing, and places to sleep. Therefore, people who were not mining for gold found work supplying the miners.

The newcomers included Chinese workers, a new wave of Mexicans, and free African

Panning for Gold

Early gold miners used simple technology to search for gold in California's rivers. You can make a sieve similar to the ones used by the forty-niners. The sieve helps to strain out gravel, leaving the gold behind.

If you have a mesh strainer in the kitchen, you can use that. If not, window screen material is inexpensive to buy.

You Will Need:

- Two foil pie pans
- Mesh screen material from a hardware store
- A knife
- Scissors
- White chalk or a pencil

People today still pan for gold using tools similar to those used during the gold rush.

Instructions:

1. Keep one of the foil pans to use as your gold pan in the later steps.
2. Cut a circle out of the bottom of the second foil pan. Ask an adult to help you start it by slitting it with a knife. Then you can stick scissors through the slit and cut in a circle. Make the circle about 6 inches (15 centimeters) in diameter, leaving a 2-inch (5 cm) frame around the bottom of the pie pan.
3. Cut the piece of screen into a circle the same size as the bottom of the foil pan. You can use the pie pan as a pattern, tracing around it with the chalk.
4. Lay the circular piece of screen in the pie pan with the circular hole in it. You now have a sieve!

How to Pan for Gold:

1. Take your pans to a gently flowing creek or stream of water.
2. Place the sieve pan within your gold pan, then scoop some gravel and silt into them both. Gently lift the sieve so that small, heavy particles can fall through into the other pan. Heavy and tiny material such as gold will fall through into the bottom pan (the "gold pan"), while the other material such as stones will remain in the sieve.
3. Set aside the sieve so that you are holding the gold pan filled with small particles. Gently swirl and see if you catch sight of a gold flake. Watch for a glimpse of a sparkle!

Americans. Some African Americans used their wealth from mining gold to buy the freedom of relatives held as slaves in the South.

Uneven Riches

The gold rush did not go on forever, but California kept growing. In 1869, a transcontinental railroad linked California with the eastern United States. The railroad made it easier for people and goods to reach the state. The business leaders who helped bring about the building of the rail lines became millionaires. However, the Chinese immigrants who did much of the actual labor of building the railroads did not get much money for their hard work.

The transcontinental railroad changed American transportation, but the workers who built it were treated terribly.

Chinese employees received twenty-seven to thirty dollars a month, which did not include the cost of food and a place to stay. Immigrants from Ireland and other "white" (European) workers were paid thirty-five dollars per month. This wage did include the cost of a place to stay. The work was dangerous. Much of it was done with hand tools. Employees worked twelve hours a day, six days a week.

California's farmland provided other jobs. Because many areas did not have enough rain to raise crops, the state began a series of irrigation projects to bring water to dry land. By the end of the nineteenth century, land was cheap and many people had the opportunity to own farms.

The 1906 earthquake caused terrible damage to the city of San Francisco.

The San Francisco Earthquake

On Wednesday, April 18, 1906, at about 5:00 a.m., an earthquake started off the coast of San Francisco and moved into the city. It lasted only about a minute, but there were

California Poppy Day

California poppies have their own holiday!

The California poppy (*Eschscholzia californica*) was chosen as the state flower in 1903. This beautiful orange-yellow flower grows wild throughout the state, lighting up the landscape like bits of gold. The leaves are delicate and fernlike. The first European naturalist to describe this flower was Adelbert von Chamisso, traveling on a Russian ship in the 1810s. Chamisso named the flower in Latin after a friend. Chamisso and his ship landed in San Francisco in 1816. There the bay was surrounded by these beautiful blooming flowers.

Long before that, however, Native Americans were using the poppy seeds as food and a source of oil. They also mixed the oil with bear fat to use as a hairstyling product. The green part of the plant was cooked as a vegetable.

Another name for this flower is *copa de oro*, which means "cup of gold" in Spanish. Gold is an important theme in California, known as the Golden State, and the state flower is no exception!

On California Poppy Day, schoolchildren in California are taught about the high value of native plants and our responsibilities to take care of our natural resources. The celebrations continue with annual festivals dedicated to the flower.

California poppies are easy to grow from seeds. Scatter the seeds on garden soil in fall or early spring. After spring rains, the flowers will bloom. No watering is needed because the flowers can tolerate drought. The flowers will close at night or on cloudy days but reopen in sun. In fact, California poppies are now grown in many places outside of California—even in English gardens!

Some people think it is illegal to pick the state flower. However, that is true only on state lands. People are allowed to pick poppies on private land. But they do not last long after being picked. It might be best to enjoy them in a garden instead of a bouquet.

seventeen aftershocks. It had an estimated magnitude of 7.8 on the Richter scale. Buildings crumbled, streets cracked apart, and **debris** flew everywhere. Gas lines broke, causing fires that raged out of control for days. In the end, more than three thousand people were killed in and near the city. Many more were injured or left homeless. But aid poured in from far and wide. Before long, the determined people of San Francisco rebuilt their city.

Mary Pickford was one of the most popular actresses of the early 1900s.

Hollywood's Movie Magic

In the early twentieth century, the movie industry was born. Filmmakers realized that the warm climate and open space of Southern California made it the perfect spot to make movies. The film industry grew up in an area of Los Angeles called Hollywood. To many, it seemed like a magical place, where dreams came to life on the screen. California drew thousands of people looking for work in the movie industry. Hollywood is still the movie capital of the world.

Hard Times

In the 1920s, California and the rest of the United States had a strong economy. After 1929, however, the country faced difficult times. During the Great Depression, many banks failed and businesses closed. People lost the money they had saved in the banks. Millions of workers lost their jobs. During the 1930s, years of drought and terrible dust storms destroyed farms and homes across the Great Plains. Hundreds of thousands of people from the region, which became known as the Dust Bowl, packed up and moved to California. They were attracted by the mild climate and long growing season. Many were treated poorly by Californians and scraped by in low-paying jobs picking cotton or fruit.

In the 1940s, World War II helped pull California and the rest of the country out of the Depression. The US government spent billions of dollars to make ships, planes, weapons, and supplies. The state was a center for those industries, and jobs in the factories and shipyards lured more people to California.

Postwar Boom

After World War II, companies that made weapons, ships, and planes continued to get work from the government. People were drawn to the state's warm weather. Many thought California had an easygoing, laid-back lifestyle. By the mid-1960s, more people lived in California than in any other state.

For some people, California was a place where they could dress, speak, and act differently from the typical American. In the 1950s, poets such as Allen Ginsberg and writers such as Jack Kerouac flocked to San Francisco and wrote about life as they saw it. These writers and others became known as "beatniks."

In the 1960s, California was the center of a so-called youth movement. The interests of teenagers and young adults shaped music and film. The Beach Boys and other California groups sang about the beach, surfing, dating, and cars.

During the 1960s, the United States became involved in a war in Vietnam, a country in Southeast Asia. Many Americans opposed the war and organized protests. At the University of California at Berkeley, students staged sits-ins in school buildings and called for changes in running the university. Many were arrested in **confrontations** with police. Meanwhile, in San Francisco, "hippies" found a home. A number of hippies wore sandals or went barefoot and grew their hair long. They preached peace and hoped for an end to the Vietnam War.

Silicon Valley's Ups and Downs

During the twentieth century, the Santa Clara Valley, south of San Francisco Bay, developed as a center for technology. The area has become known as Silicon Valley because the element silicon is commonly used to make the chips that power computers. Hewlett-Packard was started there in the late 1930s. Intel arrived in the late 1960s. In 1976, Steve Jobs and his friend Steve Wozniak founded Apple, an important computer company. In the 1990s, Yahoo! and Google were among the many internet companies that started in the valley. Today, industries that produce computers and computer software, along with internet service industries, are key parts of the state's economy.

By 2000, the computer boom was slowing. Some people who invested in high-tech companies in Silicon Valley lost much of their money. Many workers in Silicon Valley lost their jobs. Those losses meant that the state government got less money from taxes. At the same time, California's population was growing fast. The government was spending more and more money on services. California also faced a big energy crunch. As the population increased, so did the demand for electricity, but new power plants had not been built. As electricity prices rose, some businesses had to shut down because of high energy costs.

Under California law, an elected official can be removed from office and replaced by someone else in a special "recall" election. That happened

Many exciting tech companies make their home in California's Silicon Valley.

in October 2003, when voters removed Governor Gray Davis and replaced him with Arnold Schwarzenegger, a former body builder and film star who had become active in politics.

Even with a new governor, the state still had money problems. In 2008, the economy of the whole country took a downturn. In 2009, California's governor and legislature missed a deadline for approving a new **budget**. The government briefly ran out of money and had to issue IOUs (signed promises) to people who were supposed to receive checks from the state. A budget was finally adopted, and the state began to pay up. But the new budget called for big cuts in education and other services. The government still had worries about making ends meet. Governor Schwarzenegger called on the people of California to pull together and make the sacrifices needed to help solve the state's financial problems.

California has rebounded from the financial stress of the early part of this century, partly because of the large investments the state has made in new technologies. Also, the technology sector in the San Francisco Bay Area has helped pull the whole state out of its recession. But the drawback of the growing economy combined with increasing population is that housing has become very expensive. As of early 2018, Governor Jerry Brown was working hard with other branches of government to create laws and programs to make housing more affordable for the diverse people of California.

Today's Natural Disasters

In recent history, the state of California has struggled against a force beyond anyone's control: Mother Nature. Starting in 2011, the state faced its worst drought of all time. The drought lasted from December of 2011 until April of 2017. The drought had major consequences for people all over California. Farmers planted fewer crops. People had to follow strict rules about water usage. Because of dry conditions (and high temperatures), wildfires took a big toll. Californians lost their homes, and forests were destroyed. Wildfires also caused many people to lose power.

The state had to look to new dams for drinking water as the drought raged on. California's government took several steps to help citizens. First, the government created a task force. Then, state lawmakers passed a bill authorizing the government to spend almost $700 million to help Californians. Now that the drought is over, the people and government of California are deciding whether water usage rules should stay in place. Some people argue that these rules help California use a precious resource more wisely.

Important Californians

Ansel Adams

Ansel Adams

Ansel Adams was born in 1902. From San Francisco, Adams became famous for his large-scale, black-and-white photographs of spectacular natural landscapes. He did not do well in school but loved spending time in nature and playing music. His pictures of Yosemite in the Sierra Nevada brought him success and helped the national parks. He worked hard to preserve nature.

Estelle Peck Ishigo

Born in Oakland in 1899, Ishigo later married a nisei (second-generation Japanese American) man. She voluntarily joined her husband when he was held in the Pomona detention camp and at Heart Mountain camp during World War II. Her drawings, sketches, and watercolors, now in the Japanese American National Museum, show what life in the internment camps was like.

Ursula K. Le Guin

Born in 1929 in Berkeley, Le Guin is best known for her science fiction and fantasy writing, although she wrote many kinds of texts. She wrote novels, children's books, short stories, poetry, and essays. In 2014, she won the National Book Foundation's Medal for Distinguished Contribution to American Letters.

John Muir

John Muir was born in 1838. He moved from Scotland to the United States at age eleven. He loved to travel, especially by foot. At age thirty, he walked across the San Joaquin Valley! He then made his home in Yosemite. All his life, he worked to preserve nature, especially his beloved Sierra Nevada. Many places are named for him.

Mary Ellen Pleasant

Mary Ellen Pleasant was born in 1814. An African American woman, she is considered the "Mother of Civil Rights in California." She worked on the Underground Railroad to bring people to freedom. She was also a brilliant entrepreneur who used her money to **obtain** jobs and rights for African Americans. Her work earned her the name "The Black City Hall."

Mary Ellen Pleasant

Lucy Telles

Lucy Telles was born in the late 1800s. She was a Native American who kept alive her people's traditional basket-making skills, demonstrating them at Yosemite National Park. She belonged to the Mono Lake Paiute and Sierra Miwok tribes. Some of her elaborate baskets survive today and can be seen at the National Museum of the American Indian and other museums.

Ronald Reagan

Born in 1911, Reagan moved to Hollywood in 1937. He worked for a labor union for actors. In 1966, Reagan was elected governor of California. In 1980, he was elected president of the United States and served two terms. He was one of the most popular US presidents.

Lucy Telles, with one of her baskets

Jackie Robinson

Jackie Robinson was born in 1919. He was the first African American to play in Major League Baseball, starting on April 15, 1947, when he played his first game for the Brooklyn Dodgers. He played in six World Series, was an All-Star for six years in a row (from 1949 to 1954), and was inducted into the Baseball Hall of Fame. Robinson grew up in California.

Palm trees line a crowded street in Santa Monica.

3 Who Lives in California?

As of 2017, the federal government estimated California's population at more than thirty-nine million people—by far the largest population of any state. By comparison, the second most populous state, Texas, had about twenty-eight million people. California is also the most diverse state in the country. Well over one-third (about 39 percent) of all Californians are Hispanic or Latino. That means that they or their ancestors came from Mexico or another Spanish-speaking country. As of 2016, about 15 percent of Californians were Asian, about 7 percent were African American, and 14 percent were of a race not listed on the census.

A State of Immigrants

From its earliest beginnings, California has been home to a mix of different peoples. The Native American groups had differences in language and culture. They were joined—and to a large extent pushed aside—by Spanish settlers from the south and English-speaking pioneers from the east. The gold rush that started in 1848 drew a large wave of people to California from all corners of the

FAST FACT
In the 1870s, Eadweard Muybridge photographed a trotting horse in a series of images, at the request of Leland Stanford, the former governor of California. Some people describe these images as the ancestor of the motion picture (movies). Then, in 1908, a movie was made in Los Angeles. Quickly, moviemakers discovered the benefits of working in California—and the Hollywood movie industry was born.

world. After the gold rush, the state continued to attract people to work in its mines, railroads, fields, shipyards, and factories. Today, people from countries far and wide live in California and work in its service and high-tech industries.

At times, people from different groups have clashed. Native Americans, Hispanics, Asians, and African Americans have all suffered from injustice and discrimination. At the same time, all these groups have added to the culture of California and helped build the state into what it is today.

Big Cities, Big Suburbs

Although California has a lot of wide-open spaces, most of the people live clustered together in suburbs and cities. The Los Angeles–Long Beach–Anaheim metropolitan area has more than 13 million people, about one-third of the state's total population. Three California cities have populations of over 1 million.

San Diego is the eighth-largest city in America.

As of 2017, Los Angeles alone had almost 4 million people. It is the biggest city in California and the second-biggest city in the United States, behind New York City. San Diego is the second-largest California city, with over 1.4 million people. It is followed by San Jose, with over 1 million, and San Francisco, with about 884,000. Also among the top-fifty US cities in population are Fresno, Long Beach, Sacramento (California's capital), and Oakland (located next to San Francisco).

San Jose clocks in as the tenth-largest city in America.

Though California has many cities with 100,000 people or more, small towns in the desert and in the mountains have only a few hundred residents. These places can be hours away from big cities, with only a few roads and stores. Northern California, between Sacramento and Oregon, is a region the size of New York State, but it has only about 5 percent of California's residents. People say it is cheaper to live there than in the rest of California.

Latino and Hispanic Californians

Some cities are known for having a large population of a particular ethnic group. For example, Latinos make up almost half the population of Los Angeles. Most are from Mexico, but large numbers also come from, or have ancestors who came from, the Caribbean and Central and South America. But Latinos

Alcatraz is one of numerous sites in California with a Spanish name.

are not only in Los Angeles—their numbers are rising across the state. By 2016, California's population was 38.9 percent Latino/Hispanic—a slightly higher proportion than non-Latino/Hispanic whites (37.7 percent).

Many California Latinos speak both English and Spanish. The state has celebrations every year during Hispanic Heritage Month, which runs from September 15 to October 15. Californians also celebrate Cinco de Mayo (which means "fifth of May" in Spanish) to honor the Mexican army's victory over French forces in 1862.

Many places in California have Spanish names. For example, Los Angeles is Spanish for "the angels." San Francisco is named after a Spanish mission that honored Saint Francis. The city of Fresno is named after the Spanish word for "ash tree." Even Alcatraz, the island in San Francisco Bay that houses a well-known former prison, has a Spanish name. Alcatraz is the Spanish word for "strange bird" or "pelican," so named because pelicans once lived on the island.

For many years, Californians with non-Hispanic European backgrounds had nearly all the leadership roles in the state. More recently, however, Mexican Americans and other Latinos have become more active in politics and business. In 1998, Cruz Bustamante was elected lieutenant governor, the second-highest position in the state government. He was the first Latino elected to a statewide government job in 120 years. Bustamante won reelection in 2002. Another **prominent** Latino politician is Antonio

Antonio Villaraigosa served as Los Angeles's mayor—twice!

Villaraigosa, who was twice elected mayor of Los Angeles. Today, a number of California's representatives in Congress are of Hispanic or Latino descent.

Prisoners at a Japanese internment camp in California

Asians and South Asians

When the gold rush began, many Chinese people settled in cities and in small towns to farm, build the railroads, and work in mines. The Chinese and people from other Asian countries have had a lasting effect on California. For example, Japanese farmers helped turn the Central Valley into a rich agricultural area.

Life for Asian Americans, however, has not always been easy. Racism made it hard for the first Asians in California to find work. In the past, some Californians encouraged the US government to pass laws to keep more Asians from moving to the United States. Many state laws also limited the legal rights of Chinese immigrants.

During World War II, the United States and its allies fought against Japan, Germany, and their allies. Many Americans feared that Japanese Americans would not be loyal to the United States. As a result, the US government rounded up Japanese Americans and sent them to special detention facilities, called internment camps. These camps were like prisons. In 1944, the US Supreme Court ruled that the US government could not detain loyal citizens. However, "loyal citizens" was not interpreted to mean all Japanese Americans. Three other Supreme Court cases upheld the government's ability to intern Japanese Americans. By 1946, though, the camps were closed.

California today is home to many people who have roots in other countries in Asia. These include people of Indian, Chinese, Filipino,

FAST FACT

According to a 2014 report, California's aerospace industry is bigger than both its agriculture and entertainment industries combined. This is one reason why STEM education is so important in preparing students for jobs of the future. California's deserts provide plenty of open space and consistent weather for building airplanes, rockets, and other specialized equipment.

California's Biggest Colleges and Universities

(All enrollment numbers are from US News and World Report 2018 college rankings.)

California State University, Northridge

University of California, Berkeley

University of California, San Diego

1. California State University, Northridge

(35,552 undergraduate students)

2. California State University, Fullerton

(34,576 undergraduate students)

3. California State University, Long Beach

(32,246 undergraduate students)

4. University of California, Los Angeles

(30,873 undergraduate students)

5. San Diego State University

(29,853 undergraduate students)

6. University of California, Davis

(29,546 undergraduate students)

7. University of California, Berkeley

(29,311 undergraduate students)

8. University of California, San Diego

(28,127 undergraduate students)

9. California State University, Sacramento

(27,876 undergraduate students)

10. University of California, Irvine

(27,311 undergraduate students)

Japanese, Korean, and Vietnamese descent. One out of every four Asian Americans in California is from the Philippines, about the same number as those who are Chinese American. Though the state still has a large Japanese American population, there are even more people today who trace their origins to Vietnam, India, or Korea. People from each Asian group celebrate different traditional holidays. For example, every year in late January or early February, Vietnamese Americans celebrate their New Year.

Ted Lieu was elected to the House of Representatives in 2014.

In Fremont, Californians from India or whose ancestors are from India get together each year to celebrate their culture. Many women wear the traditional long garment called a sari, and everyone enjoys Indian music and food.

Asian representatives from California include Doris Matsui, Judy Chu, Ted Lieu, and Mark Takano, among others.

California's African American Influence

African Americans have lived in California since Spanish and Mexican times. Many came during the gold rush. Some came as slaves with their owners. Other African Americans arrived as free people wanting to start a new life.

Slavery was outlawed in California even before it became a state. African Americans, however, still struggled with racism. They were not treated the same as white Americans, and it made their lives more difficult. Some presented themselves as white in order to find employment. Then they used their money to help improve life for other African Americans.

Jackie Robinson was a Californian who changed baseball forever.

Many African Americans came to California during and after World War II. They often lived in poor neighborhoods of big cities. Many

Population Changes in Native American Communities

Before Europeans arrived, Native Americans were the only people in California. The Spanish brought diseases to California that killed many of the Natives. European and American settlers also pushed the Native people off their lands. Historians believe there were once at least 300,000 Native Americans in California. By the late nineteenth century, there were fewer than 30,000. However, numbers have risen since then. Today, more than 719,300 Californians identify themselves as Native American or part Native American. That is more individuals than in any other state. On the other hand, some states other than California have a greater proportion compared to their total population, such as Alaska (19.5 percent), Oklahoma (12.9 percent), and New Mexico (10.7 percent).

Many California Native Americans live on reservations set aside for their tribes. Some prefer to call themselves American Indians. These people have their own governments and laws, but they are also US citizens. Of course, language plays a big part in Native American cultures. It is difficult to tell for sure how many languages Native American tribes spoke before California became a state. However, experts believe that there were around one hundred tribal languages. Many of these languages are dying out. Tribes and nonprofit groups are working toward preserving as many Native languages as they can.

Many people on reservations face poverty. Yet many American Indians have set up their own successful businesses to increase their income and reduce poverty. The rate of poverty has been slowly falling, while the number of Native people attending colleges and universities has increased in recent years.

Native Americans in California and elsewhere in the United States are often advocates for better environmental practices. They ask local, state, and federal governments to use more responsible actions when managing natural resources.

African Americans also had trouble getting good jobs. Despite their struggles, African Americans from California have made important contributions to all areas of society. Baseball great Jackie Robinson grew up in Pasadena. In 1947, he began playing for the Brooklyn Dodgers, breaking the color barrier that had kept African Americans out of Major League Baseball. In 1973, Los Angeles elected its first African American mayor, Tom Bradley. He held the position for twenty years. Several other California cities have since elected black mayors. Today, Maxine Waters is a well-known congresswoman from California who happens to be black. And in 2016, Kamala Harris, from California, was the second African American woman to be elected to the US Senate.

Tom Bradley was Los Angeles's first African American mayor.

Better Together

Ensuring that all Californians have equal rights and live together peacefully is one of the state's big challenges. In recent years, every ethnic group has faced tough times. But for people from many parts of the world, California remains a land of opportunity.

Both old and new groups can be respected. For example, the city of Los Angeles decided in 2017 to rename Columbus Day as Indigenous Peoples Day. People worked together to reach an agreement about the new holiday.

As activist Cesar Chavez said, "Preservation of one's own culture does not require contempt or disrespect for other cultures." With respect and care, Californians will celebrate the unique qualities of all the state's cultures.

FAST FACT

Steve Jobs and Steve Wozniak worked together in the Jobs family garage to design and build the first personal computer, the Apple I. Jobs had to sell his vehicle and Wozniak sold a Hewlett-Packard calculator in order to raise enough money to build their first twenty-five computers to sell.

Sourdough Bread

Because yeast was hard to come by in the early days of the West, sourdough bread became a popular and tasty alternative. It relies on wild yeast and bacteria that live in the air to make the bread rise and give it a deliciously tart taste.

In order to make sourdough bread, you need to have sourdough starter, which you can purchase, get from a friend, or start yourself. Once you have your starter, you can keep it alive in the fridge and "feed" it twice a week. Always save some of your starter to keep growing. Use the rest in your bread.

For the Starter

- 5 cups of all-purpose flour
- 2 ½ cups of water

1. Starting sourdough yourself will take about five days. Place 1 cup all-purpose flour and ½ cup of water in a glass jar. Stir well, then cover the container loosely with the lid or a cloth with a rubber band around it, and wait twenty-four hours.
2. The next day, you might see some bubbles in it, which means that wild yeast has started to live in it. Throw away half the starter, then feed the remainder with 1 cup flour and ½ cup water. Again, mix well, cover, and wait twenty-four hours.
3. Continue the process until your starter has a tangy but fresh odor. Each day, the starter becomes stronger as it continues to feed. To make the starter even stronger, you can feed it twice a day if you have time. (If you don't want to throw away the extra starter, you can mix it into pancakes or pizza dough instead. But if you keep it all going for five days, you will end up with a giant mountain of it in your kitchen!)

For the Bread

- 2 cups starter
- 1 teaspoon brown sugar
- ¼ cup cool water
- 3 cups bread flour
- 1 teaspoon salt
- Oil
- Cornmeal (enough to sprinkle on a baking sheet)

1. Mix the starter, brown sugar, water, flour, and salt together in a bowl. You can use a kitchen mixer if you have one. Coat your hands with oil and knead for a few minutes. Shape into a round loaf.
2. Sprinkle a baking sheet with cornmeal, then place your loaf on it. Let rise for three to five hours until doubled in size. (If you don't want to wait so long, you can add 2 teaspoons instant-rise yeast to the dough. The flavor will be a little different, but still tasty.)
3. Preheat the oven to 425 degrees Fahrenheit. Ask an adult to help you use a sharp knife to make two slashes in the top of the loaf. Bake for twenty-five to thirty minutes until golden brown, then cool. Serve with real butter or grape jelly or orange marmalade.

The Celebrities of California

Dwayne Johnson

Joan Didion

Joan Didion is well known for her personal essays and nonfiction books. Some of her work is about being from California.

Dwayne "The Rock" Johnson

Dwayne Johnson was known as "The Rock" when he was a professional wrestler. He is also an actor, producer, and former college football player. You might have heard him as the voice of Polynesian demigod Maui in the Disney film *Moana*. Johnson was born in Hayward, California.

Rashida Jones

Rashida Jones was born in Los Angeles and went on to attend Harvard University. Jones is an actress, producer, singer, songwriter, and comic book author.

Kendrick Lamar

Kendrick Lamar is a musician and writer from Compton, California. His music explores his home neighborhood and community. He writes about problems in the world such as racial discrimination and gang violence. In 2018, he won the Pulitzer Prize for Music.

Kendrick Lamar

Adam Levine

Adam Levine, from Los Angeles, is the lead singer for the band Maroon 5. He has raised awareness about attention deficit hyperactivity disorder (ADHD), which he has.

Katy Perry

Katy Perry began her career by singing gospel music in church and is now among the world's most famous pop stars. Perry was born and raised in California.

Katy Perry

George Takei

George Takei played the character Hikaru Sulu on the television series *Star Trek* and is well known on social media. He works for LGBT rights and builds positive relationships between Japan and the United States through the Japanese American National Museum. Takei is from Los Angeles.

Venus Williams

Venus Williams was born in Lynwood in 1980. Both Venus and her sister Serena are tennis champions. (Serena was born in Michigan but was raised in California.) Venus has won several Wimbledon titles and Olympic gold medals. In addition to being a tennis superstar, Venus is an entrepreneur.

Zendaya

Zendaya is a dancer, singer, actress, and model from Oakland. She starred as Rocky Blue in *Shake It Up*, a Disney channel sitcom.

Zendaya

California's climate is
ideal for growing produce,
like these strawberries.

4 At Work in California

P eople use numbers to try to explain the value of things. Economists are people who try to calculate the worth of work, products, and resources. California's economy is ranked as the sixth largest in the world, with just five countries in the world producing more wealth. One of those countries is the whole United States! California's economy is strong because of its agriculture, its incredible water and irrigation infrastructure, Silicon Valley, its natural resources, and the creativity of its people.

The total value of goods and services produced in California is about $2.46 trillion, according to *Forbes*. That is about 14 percent of all goods and services produced in the whole United States. No other state comes close to producing as much.

The Salad Bowl of the World

When Americans munch on almonds or walnuts, they are usually eating food that was grown in

California is a leading producer of walnuts.

California. The state's farmers also grow almost all the artichokes, figs, olives, and clingstone peaches eaten in the United States. California farmers lead in the production of many other products. These include milk, grapes, lettuce, strawberries, broccoli, lemons, carrots, celery, and alfalfa hay.

California is by far the number-one agricultural state in the country. Each year, its farms grow and sell crops, livestock, and other agricultural products worth well over $47 billion. These foods end up on kitchen tables around the globe. The Salinas Valley, one of the major farming regions in California, has been called the "salad bowl of the world" because of the many types of vegetables grown there.

To harvest crops, California farmers rely heavily on migrant workers. These workers travel to different farms when and where they are needed. Some come from Mexico each day to work and then return home at night. Others live in California, harvesting different crops at different times of the year. Many of the workers came across the border—to get work and earn money for their families—without having obtained the necessary US government documents giving them the right to enter the country. These people are known as "undocumented" immigrants. US law **prohibits** the hiring of undocumented workers. However, many employers ignore the law. In some cases, employers pay undocumented workers lower wages than other workers. They also give them poorer working conditions because employers know the undocumented laborers will not complain to government authorities. Migrant workers have difficult lives. Luckily, many Californians are working to improve the migrants' living and working conditions.

Another big problem for California farming is finding enough water. Farms use the largest share of the state's water. In recent years, the demand for water by farmers and residents has grown, but the supply of water has not. The state has also suffered from periods of drought that have lasted for years. These dry weather

These free-range chickens live in Northern California.

FAST FACT

Since 2005, the number of Mexican immigrants coming to the United States has decreased. In 2017, a labor shortage caused some farmers to turn to robotic farm equipment to do some of the jobs that human workers used to do. For example, Driscoll uses an Agrobot machine to pick strawberries, although it misses one out of three berries.

Workers pick lettuce at a Salinas farm.

Droughts are a common concern among California farmers. Here, soy crops struggle during a drought.

conditions have helped cause many dangerous wildfires that destroy homes and crops.

Resources from the Earth

Mining is very important in California. The state's miners dig up metals and rocks that are used to make products or building materials. These include sand and gravel used in construction and cement.

Boron is produced from borax mines, like this one.

Californians drill deep into the ground and under the water offshore to take out petroleum and natural gas. California is the only state that produces boron, which is used to make some types of soap. The state also still mines gold, but mining is not as prominent as producing wind and solar power. One of the world's largest solar power plants is located in California's Mojave Desert. However, California must import much of the electricity it needs from other states. For this reason, and because of weather conditions and other factors, the state has had energy problems. In 2000 and 2001, the state experienced blackouts that left many people without electricity. The price of electricity became very high.

Gold miners display a small finding in Alleghany, California.

Another important natural resource is timber. California has more forest land than

any other state except Alaska and Oregon. Most of the trees used for paper, lumber, and other wood products come from Northern California. In 2015, the US set records for exporting forest products to China, Canada, and Mexico. Some state residents want limits on cutting trees, since logging can destroy homes for wildlife and cause the erosion (wearing away) of soil. Also, there are not as many large trees as there once were. Others argue that limits on logging may hurt lumber companies and cause a loss of jobs. Newer, science-based methods of logging can reduce the amount of harm to the environment compared to older methods like clear-cutting.

The Ivanpah Solar Electric Generating System is in the Mojave Desert.

This oil rig is located off the California coast.

Goods and Services

When people in foreign countries buy a product made in America, there is a good chance the item came from California. The state is one of the biggest exporters of goods (in terms of value) in the United States. These include cars, processed foods, and dozens of other products. California is also a leader in the aerospace industry. Aerospace companies make airplanes and spacecraft. Californians still make much of the equipment that sends people into space or flies them across the country and around the world.

A logging company hauls away trees after a fire.

At Work in California • 61

The Pants of the Gold Rush

Levi Strauss (1829–1902)

California is rare among states for having its own designated state fabric: denim. Governor Jerry Brown signed the bill for this state symbol in September 2016. Although the fabric originally came out of the sixteenth and seventeenth centuries in Italy and France, it gained a special place in history during the gold rush. Levi Strauss came to California in 1853 hoping to strike riches in gold. He ended up finding his fortune a different way—as a dry-goods merchant selling blankets and supplies to new settlers and miners throughout the West.

Levi Strauss teamed up with a tailor from Nevada named Jacob Davis who had figured out how to reinforce pants pockets and other weak areas with copper rivets. Together, they got a patent for "Improvement in Fastening Pocket-Openings." After their first pair was made and patented in 1873, Levi's blue jeans quickly became very popular with hard-working people because the fabric was so strong—and the pants had strong pockets!

Miners wore them as they panned for gold, and they sometimes washed them in the river. Back then, the pants were called "waist overalls." They weren't called "jeans" until the 1950s.

In 1918, Levi's designed its first garment intended for women, a tunic with trousers called "Freedom-Alls." Working women in the West needed clothing in which they could move freely and do their work. In 1934, Levi's designed a pair of jeans especially for women, who had already been wearing men's jeans for years.

Levi's was the first jeans brand. Today, Levi's is still the top denim company, reporting $4.75 billion in sales in 2015. Their familiar red tag and the arched design embroidered on the back pockets are trademarked.

Today, 75 percent of the world's designer jeans come from California, and 98 percent of all American-made jeans are manufactured in San Francisco or Los Angeles.

Wealth in Silicon Valley

Apple's headquarters in Cupertino

The area around San Jose is known as Silicon Valley. Silicon is a material used to make computer chips. The area has many companies that make computer hardware and software. Apple is one of many such companies based there. Silicon Valley and San Francisco are also home to many of the biggest internet companies. Google and Yahoo! have headquarters there, as do eBay and the social-networking site Facebook.

The Hospitality Industry

The largest part of California's economy is the service industry. This includes such businesses as hotels, restaurants, banks and other financial institutions, retail stores, and insurance

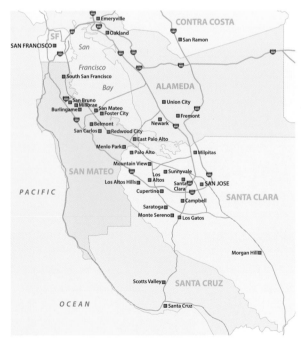

Parts of San Mateo County, Santa Clara County, and Alameda County make up Silicon Valley.

New and Emerging Industries in California

It's an exciting time for many new industries in California. Some new things to watch as they develop include electric cars, self-driving cars, better solar power, and other types of clean energy sources.

Electric cars are not a new idea. However, more people than ever are working to develop them into practical, efficient vehicles. Both gas-electric hybrid cars and fully electric cars are getting better with each new model.

Many people think that self-driving cars will make people safer and may also reduce the amount of energy needed for travel. Problems like long commutes and accidents might be reduced by this new solution. Much work is still needed to make these cars safe and practical. This means jobs for engineers, traffic experts, programmers, safety inspectors, and a host of other workers.

California is at the front of "green" technology. In fact, after the United States federal government decided to bow out of the Paris Climate Agreement in summer 2017, California and several other states stepped up to help. Governor Jerry Brown of California met in Beijing with President Xi Jingping of China in June 2017. They pledged to expand trade on green technologies to help address one of the biggest problems of today: climate change.

Silicon Valley continues to play a vital role in sustaining California's economy. Just think of the latest iPhone, the Fitbit, the Apple Watch, and other gadgets that people buy to help them improve their work and health, or for entertainment.

Governor Brown met with China's president, Xi Jingping, in 2017.

Designing these devices, along with their software and applications, requires the hard work of many people. Developing tech products provides hundreds of jobs for people working in the fields of technology, computers, and programming. Other jobs arise, too, such as in graphic design, marketing, and even packaging, to make the products appealing to buyers.

The San Diego Zoo is home to thousands of animals and exotic plants.

companies. Hospitals and schools are also part of the service sector. Two other important industries in California are tourism and film production.

Tourism adds over $100 billion to the state's economy each year. People from all over the world come to explore Los Angeles, San Francisco, and other cities. Animal lovers flock to the San Diego Zoo, one of the most famous zoos in the world. Nature enthusiasts enjoy the natural beauty of Yosemite, Redwood, Sequoia, and California's five other national parks. Visitors are also attracted to the state's scenic coastline and sandy beaches. Disneyland and other well-known theme parks attract fun-loving visitors of all ages.

Disneyland opened in 1955.

Filmmakers create movies and television shows. Los Angeles is the center of the film-production industry. Entertainment companies have studios in the region, where they film movies and TV shows.

The Hollywood
Walk of Fame

The entertainment industry alone brings in billions of dollars each year.

The 2028 Olympics

It's not just permanent attractions that draw visitors to California. Aside from Hollywood and Disneyland, sometimes special events bring tourists from all over the world. In 2017, California state government officials and officials from the International Olympic Committee (IOC) reached an agreement. That agreement named Los Angeles as the host of the 2028 Olympic and Paralympic Games. In exchange for hosting the Olympics, Los Angeles will receive a payment of about $2 billion from the IOC. This will be the third time Los Angeles has hosted the Olympics. Previously, the city hosted in 1932 and 1984. The 2028 Games are an excellent opportunity for businesses in California to thrive. Visitors to Los Angeles will bring revenue as they eat, shop, and stay in hotels to watch Olympians compete.

The Education Sector

Education is very important in California—and a big part of the economy. California has more than 10,000 public elementary and secondary schools, with about 295,000 teachers and more than 6.2 million students—more than any other state.

California is also noted for its system of public colleges and universities. The University of California has ten campuses around the state, including UC Berkeley and UCLA. In addition, the California State University system has twenty-three campuses, including Cal State Fullerton and Fresno State. California has a large network of community colleges as well.

California is also home to many fine private colleges and universities, such as

Stanford University and the California Institute of Technology (Caltech). The University of Southern California, or USC, is another well-known private university. It has long been a rival school to its crosstown neighbor, UCLA.

Stanford is one of California's prestigious private universities.

Challenges for the Economy

The state was hard hit by the recession, or economic downturn, that affected the whole country by 2008. State and local governments in California had a difficult time balancing their budgets and paying for education and other services for a growing population. Home values fell sharply, while the unemployment rate soared. In December 2009, more than 12 percent of workers were out of a job. That was higher than the national average of 10 percent for that month. During 2009, more than 579,000 workers in California lost their jobs. In the years since, however, unemployment has dropped and home prices have soared. Skyrocketing home prices create a new problem of families being unable to afford housing, even when they have good-paying jobs.

Overall, California's wealth has grown as a result of rich natural resources combined with a diverse population of hard-working and creative people. Over time, Golden State creative thinkers have solved many problems, and they will continue to do so.

The California State Capitol Building in Sacramento is where lawmakers do the hard work of governing the state.

5 Government

Often, California poses many challenges to those who govern it because of its large size. This has sometimes created political tension. However, California has a history of giving voters a strong voice regardless. Voters propose laws, express opinions, and even recall public officials. For example, in 2003, the voters of California recalled Governor Gray Davis before his term had ended. They elected Arnold Schwarzenegger in his place.

Local Politics

California's towns and cities have governments that handle local affairs and pass local laws. As of 2010, the state had 482 cities and towns. Local citizens elect **councils** to run their cities and towns. Most cities also have mayors.

The towns and cities of California are located in fifty-eight counties. In most counties, voters elect a board of supervisors. The supervisors act like business managers who try to do what

FAST FACT

Although women make up about half the population, they do not make up half the government. According to the Center for American Women and Politics at Rutgers University, women held about 23 percent of government offices in 2016. California has helped start shifting the balance. In 1992, voters elected not one, but two female senators: Barbara Boxer and Dianne Feinstein.

is best for the county. Other county jobs include sheriff, county clerk, school **superintendent**, and district attorney. Voters elect people for all these positions.

Some counties in California have "home rule." This means they can write documents called charters, which are like local constitutions. The charters give county officials more control over how their county is run. Dozens of cities in California also have home rule.

Gray Davis was the thirty-seventh governor of California.

California's State Lawmakers

The state legislature makes laws for all Californians. The state's lawmakers, or legislators, belong to one of two houses: the state assembly or the state senate. They are elected by the voters from their district. All California voters also elect the governor and some other major state officials.

Branches of Government

Executive

This branch includes the governor, lieutenant governor, secretary of state, treasurer, and attorney general. People who hold these offices are chosen in elections. The governor has a four-year term and can serve only two terms in a row. The governor appoints many other people who help run the government. He or she also prepares a proposed budget every year. The governor and the legislature eventually have to agree on the final budget.

Arnold Schwarzenegger became governor in 2003 when Gray Davis was removed from office after a recall election.

Legislative

The state assembly and state senate make up the legislative branch. Legislators propose and pass laws for the state. Legislators can serve up to twelve years total. They can serve that time in one house, or split the time between the two houses.

Judicial

The courts are run by judges. They decide criminal or civil cases, often with the help of a jury. In criminal cases, people accused of a crime go on trial to determine whether they are guilty. In civil cases, one person or group sues another. The court then decides which side is right. Sometimes courts must also decide whether a certain law is legal under the California constitution. The judicial system includes different levels of courts. The loser in a case can appeal to a higher court. Some appeals are heard by the state's highest court, the Supreme Court of California. The governor selects judges for the supreme court. However, voters must approve judges in the first regular election after they are appointed. They need to be approved again every twelve years.

The Governor's Mansion is in Sacramento.

Federal Representation

California voters also elect people to represent them in the US Congress. There are two houses

Your State, Your Representatives

One way to participate in government is to learn more about your representatives. You can identify who your representatives are by going to the following website: https://www.govtrack.us/congress/members/CA.

The GovTrack website helps you learn more about your representatives.

There you will find your two senators and all your representatives in the House. If you click on a representative's name, you will find links to his or her official website and voting history. You can sign up to get alerts, and clicking on the "contact her" or "contact him" button lets you communicate directly with your representative. You may also ask an adult to show you your representative's Twitter or Facebook accounts.

Other useful government websites include:

http://findyourrep.legislature.ca.gov

http://www.legislature.ca.gov/legislators_and_districts/legislators/your_legislator.html

http://www.ca.gov

of Congress, the Senate and the House of Representatives. Every state has two US senators. In the House, the number of representatives from each state depends on the state's population. That number can change every ten years after the latest US census. In 2017, California had fifty-three representatives in the House. That is more than any other state because California has the largest state population.

Important decisions are made in California courtrooms, like this one.

From Bill to Law

In the California legislature, a bill, or proposed law, can be introduced by an assembly member or a senator. The bill first goes to a committee, which invites the public to comment on it. If the committee votes to approve the measure, the whole assembly or senate reviews the bill and debates its points. If one house of the legislature approves the bill, it goes to the other house. If the second house makes any changes to the bill, it must go back to the first house. In some cases, members from each house get together to make changes that both houses can agree upon. Most bills need only a majority vote to pass, but budget measures or bills that raise taxes must be approved by a two-thirds vote.

Once a bill is approved by both houses, it goes to the governor, who can either sign it into law or veto (reject) it. If the governor does not take any action on the bill, it becomes a law. If the governor vetoes the bill, it can still become a law if two-thirds of the members of both the state assembly and the state senate vote to override the veto.

For the People, By the People

State senators from different parties must work together to pass laws. This 2009 photo shows Democratic senator Denise Ducheny (*left*) and Republican senator Dennis Hollingsworth (*right*) talking about the state budget.

California has a process that lets citizens propose and pass laws and even make changes to the state's constitution. This is called the initiative process. California voters have passed initiative measures covering many issues, including taxes, term limits, and wildlife protection.

At the local level, citizens have many ways to get involved in politics. They can serve on boards that oversee schools, libraries, and parks.

High school students in San Francisco elect their own representatives to the board of education. The student representatives help the school board learn more about issues that concern students. People can also work to help candidates running for election to local or state office. In addition, citizens can work together to get an initiative on the ballot in local as well as statewide elections.

The purpose of government is to do the daily work that is needed to keep a society functioning. California's government has often been successful at meeting the needs of its citizens by providing funding for education, health care, and infrastructure like roads and bridges. It is the job of citizens to pay attention to whether their government is meeting the needs of its people. It's important to communicate with leaders and the public about positive solutions.

Glossary

budget	An official statement from a government about how much money it plans to spend during a particular period of time and how it will pay for what it needs.
confrontation	A situation in which people or groups fight or challenge each other in an angry way.
council	A groups of people who are chosen to make rules, laws, or decisions about something.
debris	The pieces that are left after something has been destroyed.
fable	A short story that is meant to teach the reader a lesson.
immigrant	A person who comes to a country to live there.
invest	To commit money in order to earn a financial return.
irrigation	The watering of land by artificial means to foster plant or crop growth.
leach	To use a liquid in order to separate out a substance.
legal	Of or relating to the law.
mission	A place that is dependent on a larger religious organization for direction or financial support.
obtain	To gain something, usually by planned action or effort.
prohibit	To prevent from doing something.
prominent	Important or well known.
silicon	A chemical element that is found in Earth's crust and is used in computers and electronics.
superintendent	A person who directs or manages a place, department, or organization.

Point
St. George
Modoc
National
Forest
Goose
Lake

KLAMATH
Redwood
National Park
MOUNTAINS
Eureka
Shasta
Lake
Cape
Mendocino
Redding
Lassen Volcanic
National Park
Punta
Gorda
Mendocino
National
Forest
Chico
Plumas
National Forest
Santa
Rosa
Yuba
City
Marshall
Gold Discovery
State Historic Park
Truckee
Lake
Tahoe
Eldorado
National Forest
Point Reyes
Sacramento
Berkeley
Stockton
San Francisco
San Francisco
Bay
Oakland
Fremont
Modesto
Mono
Lake
San
Jose
Yosemite
National Park
Santa Cruz
Monterey
Bay
Salinas
Kings Canyon
National Park
Fresno
Monterey
Mount
Whitney
Death Valley
National Park
San Luis
Obispo
Bakersfield
MOJAVE
PACIFIC
Los Padres
National
Forest
Edwards
Air Force Base
Mojave
Nationa
Preserve
Barstow
OCEAN
Point Conception
SANTA YNEZ MTS.
Santa
Clarita
Palmdale
DESERT
Joshua Tre
National
Santa Barbara
Santa Barbara Chan.
Oxnard
Glendale
San
Bernadino
Riverside
San Miguel
Santa
Rosa
Santa Cruz
Channel Islands
National Park
Los Angeles
Long
Beach
Disneyland
Anaheim
Irvine
Santa Ana
Cleveland
National Forest
Salton
Sea
Anza-Borrego
Desert State Pa
CHANNEL
Santa
Catalina
Gulf of
Oceanside
Santa Catalina
Escondido
Cleveland
National
Forest
San Nicolas
ISLANDS
San
Clemente
San
Diego
El Centro
Chula Vista

PACIFIC

OCEAN

Interstate
Highest Point
in State
State Forest
Major
Highway
Mountains
National Park
City or Town
Historic
Site
State Park
State Capital
National Forest
Other Points of Interest

N
W E
S

0   miles   150

76 • California

California State Map and Map Skills

Map Skills

1. What park is closest to the state capital?

2. What is the highest point in the state?

3. What is the westernmost city or town on this map?

4. What lake is north of Lake Tahoe?

5. Plumas National Forest is in which mountain range?

6. What interstate runs north to south?

7. What city is south of San Diego?

8. To get from Needles to Blythe, what highway would you take?

9. What point of interest is north of Palmdale?

10. To get to Cleveland National Forest from El Centro, which direction would you travel?

Answers

1. Marshall Gold Discovery State Park
2. Mount Whitney
3. Eureka
4. Goose Lake
5. Sierra Nevada
6. I-5
7. Chula Vista
8. 95
9. Edwards Air Force Base
10. West

Further Information

Books

DK Travel. *DK Eyewitness Travel Guide: California.* New York: DK, 2016.

Duffield, Katy S. *California History for Kids: Missions, Miners, and Moviemakers in the Golden State.* Chicago: Chicago Review Press, 2012.

Friedman, Mel. *The California Gold Rush.* New York: Scholastic, 2010.

Marsh, Carole. *The Mystery on the California Mission Trail.* Peachtree City, GA: Gallopade International, 2011.

Websites

The California Missions
http://californiamissionsfoundation.org/the-california-missions
Explore a map of missions in California and find information about visiting these historic sites.

Kids Connect with California AG
https://www.cdfa.ca.gov/Kids
The California Department of Food and Agriculture hosts a comprehensive website for students. Learn more about the insects, animals, and crops of California.

Visit California
http://www.visitcalifornia.com
The official website for the California Department of Tourism has pictures, maps, and a calendar of events.

Index

Page numbers in **boldface** are illustrations. Entries in **boldface** are glossary terms.